PALEO SLOW COOKER

Everyday Recipes for Stress-free Cooking and Weight Loss

(Uncovered With Your Top Paleo Diet Questions Uncovered)

Brian Smith

Published by Sharon Lohan

© Brian Smith

All Rights Reserved

Paleo Slow Cooker: Everyday Recipes for Stress-free Cooking and Weight Loss (Uncovered With Your Top Paleo Diet Questions Uncovered)

ISBN 978-1-990334-10-8

All rights reserved. No part of this guide may be reproduced in any form without permission in writing from the publisher except in the case of brief quotations embodied in critical articles or reviews.

Legal & Disclaimer

The information contained in this book is not designed to replace or take the place of any form of medicine or professional medical advice. The information in this book has been provided for educational and entertainment purposes only.

The information contained in this book has been compiled from sources deemed reliable, and it is accurate to the best of the Author's knowledge; however, the Author cannot guarantee its accuracy and validity and cannot be held liable for any errors or omissions. Changes are periodically made to this book. You must consult your doctor or get professional medical advice before using any of the suggested remedies, techniques, or information in this book.

Table of contents

Part 1	1
What is Paleo Diet?	2
Paleo Slow Cooker Recipes	8
Soups	8
Moroccan Soup with Lentils and Tomatoes	8
Miso Soup with Peas and Carrots	10
Crab Meat in Creamy Sherry Sauce	11
Onion Soup	12
Meaty Beet and Carrot Soup	13
Minestrone Soup	14
Chicken Lemon Soup with Kale	16
Sweet Potato Basil Soup	17
Main Dish	18
Seafood	18
Salmon Fillet in Maple Sauce	18
Zesty Lime Salmon with Cilantro	19
Creamy Salmon Flakes with Sweet Potatoes	20
Bacon-wrapped Eel in Red Wine Sauce	21
Tilapia Fillet with Lemon Mayo Sauce	23
Citrus Fish	24
Spicy Shrimp Stew	25
Spicy Jambalaya with Cajun	26
Beef	28
Beef Stew	28
Beef Strips in Mongolian Sauce	30
Roast Beef in Coffee Sauce	31

Beef Broccoli 32
Beef Heart with Carrots in Red Wine Sauce 33
Seasoned Pot Roast with Green Chilies 34
Roast Beef in Pepper Sauce 35
Steak in Mushroom Gravy 36
Corned Beef and Cabbage 37
Beef and Eggplant Stew 38
Meatloaf with Worcestershire Sauce 40
Lamb 41
Herbed Lamb Roast 41
Herbed Lamb Shanks with Carrots 42
Lamb Shank Curry with Pumpkin 43
Chicken 45
Chicken Wraps with Sour Cream 45
Chicken Stew in Tomato Sauce 47
Chicken Mushroom in Tomatillo Salsa 49
Kung Pao Chicken 51
Chicken with Broccoli 53
Chicken with Sweet Potatoes 55
Peppered Chicken Cacciatore 56
Zesty Lemon Chicken 57
Chicken Adobo 58
Cheesy Chicken with Mangoes in Coconut Milk 59
Chicken with Honey Soy Sauce 60
Chicken with Belgian Endive in Apple Sauce 61
Cilantro Chicken 62
Chicken in Red Curry Sauce 64
Sweet Chicken Fillet with Dijon Mustard 65

Chicken with Cabbage Kimchi ... 66
Sweet Chicken Wings ... 67
Pork ... 68
Herbed Pork Roast with Dijon Mustard ... 68
Short Ribs in Korean BBQ Sauce ... 69
Tender Pork with Apples in Maple Orange Sauce ... 71
Honey Pork Lettuce Wraps ... 72
Pulled Pork with Pineapples ... 74
Honey Apple Pork Tenderloin ... 75
Pork Loin in Butternut Squash Stew ... 76
Garlic Mashed Cauliflower ... 77
Cannellini Beans with Sage ... 78
Sweet Potato Quittata with Coconut Milk ... 79
Desserts ... 80
Banana Loaf ... 80
Cinnamon Apple Bread Pudding ... 81
Honey Glazed Banana Foster ... 82
Sweet Apple Cinnamon Jam ... 83
Part 2 ... 84
Introduction ... 85
Chapter 1 – Paleo Breakfast Recipes in ... 88
Slow Cooker ... 88
Paleo Breakfast Pie ... 89
Casserole in Slow Cooker ... 91
Low-carb Casserole ... 93
Cabbage and Apple Treat ... 95
Cinnamon Pancake ... 97
Chapter 2– Paleo Starters and Snacks ... 99

Applesauce Chicken 100

Chicken Tacos 101

Spinach Frittata 103

Roast Beef 105

Spicy Chicken 107

Chapter 3 – Paleo Stews and Soup Recipes 109

Vegetable Curry/Korma 110

Lamb Stew 112

Beef Stew 114

Chicken Tortilla Soup 116

Vegetable and Beans Soup 118

Chapter 4 – Paleo Chicken Recipes in 119

Slow Cooker 119

Salsa Chicken 121

Chicken Cacciatore 123

Roast Chicken 125

Chicken Chili 127

Chicken and Mushroom Gravy 129

Chapter 5 – Paleo Dessert Recipes 130

Glazed Pecans 131

Apple Pie Sauce 133

Brownie Bites 135

Beef Tongue with Roasted Pepper Sauce 137

Bouef Bourgignon 139

Braised Lamb Shanks & Eggplant 140

Breakfast Frittata 142

Butternut Squash Soup 143

Carnitas on Red Pepper Nachos 144

Sweet Potato Mash with Pecans 145
Cauliflower Mashed Potatoes with Garlic & Dill 147
Celery Hearts with Creamed Kale 148
Cheater's Pork Stew... 150
Conclusion.. 152

Part 1

What is Paleo Diet?

I'm pretty sure you've heard about Paleo diet somewhere. It has many names --- some people call it caveman diet while others refer to it as Stone Age or hunter-gatherer diet. So what's the theory behind Paleo Diet? It's actually pretty simple --- eat like a caveman. That means no processed food, cereals, grains, candies, dairy products, potatoes and more! If a caveman who lived a thousand years ago couldn't eat it, then you can't too. In general, Paleo Diet rids you of any modern food --- anything that comes in a jar, box or plastic bag. It helps you cut down on your carbohydrates, sugars and salts. This diet program is based on the idea that the best diet for our bodies should be made up of foods which we are most genetically adapted to – eating foods which our body is designed to eat. For more than 100,000 years, our ancestors had thrived living only on naturally-occurring food products. The discovery of agriculture 10,000 years ago, changed our eating habits from "Paleolithic" to carb-obsessed meals. Not to mention the slew of sugars and additives that comes from processed meals that we eat each day.

How Does Paleo Diet Works?

The main goal of Paleo Diet is to control the body's insulin levels. Depending on the food we eat, our insulin levels can go up or down. Why insulin? Insulin do a lot of awesome things. For instance, it regulates cholesterol, controls the storage of fat, and directs the flow of carbs and fatty acids to tissues. Uncontrolled levels of insulin, however, has detrimental effects on the body --- inability to absorb nutrients and remove excess fats, diabetes, heart disease (and more) --- to name a few. What food group greatly affects the body's insulin levels? Carbohydrates! *(Note: fats has no effect at all while protein has a very minimal effect)* Eating too much carbs causes your blood sugar and insulin (consequently) to spike. Consistent spiking makes your body insulin resistant which means that your pancreas can no longer tell how much insulin is being produced. And that's bad.

So What Can I Eat?

Naturally-occurring foods are at the heart of Paleo Diet. Below is a list that summarizes what you can eat:

• Fish – It is highly recommended that you avoid eating farmed fish as they may contain mercury and other toxins.

• Meat – Make sure that the meat was obtained from grass-fed livestock as grains causes the same adverse effects in animals too.

• Fowl – Duck, hen, chicken, turkey, etc.

• Eggs –Those that are rich in Omega-3 are highly recommended.

- Vegetables – Anything! You can eat as much as you want as long as the veggies are not deep-fried.

- Nuts – Perfect for snacks since they are rich in calories. But make sure not to eats bags of them!

- Oils – Any natural oils will do. Perfect examples are avocado oil, olive oil and coconut oil.

- Fruits – Good source of natural sugar. Don't eat too much if you are trying to lose weight.

- Tubers – Great examples are sweet potatoes and yams (stay away from potatoes!). Keep in mind that tubers are high in carbohydrates and calories so make sure you only eat enough. They're best as after workout meals.

Health Benefits of Paleo Diet

Is caveman diet a fad? Why is it so popular today? Well, it's because Paleo Diet has a lot of health benefits! Let's talk about some them.

A Truckload of Nutrients

Many critics think that Paleo Diet is all about fats and proteins. Is it? No! Paleo Diet gives your body a truckload of nutrients. These minerals and vitamins come from vegetables, nuts, fruits, seeds and healthy fats! And you know what's even better? Since you don't eat a lot grains and legumes, your digestive system becomes more efficient in absorbing nutrients from the food you eat --- making the most out of every bite!

Say Goodbye to Bloating and Gas

Research shows that people who eats paleo experience less bloating and gas. This is due to the high fiber, low-sodium food intake which keeps your gut clean and healthy.

Better Weight Loss

Paleo Diet improves your overall gut and metabolic health. It helps you sleep better thus helping you manage stress more effectively. The proper balance between Omega-3 and Omega-6 fatty acids make fat burning more efficient too! And you know what's better? There are no restrictions as to how much you should eat and when you should eat it! Since Paleo Diet is devoid of any carbs, unhealthy sugars, salts and additives, there are no risks of accumulating unhealthy fats.

Healthy Cells

Most cells in the body are made from saturated and unsaturated fats. How healthy and efficient your cells are depends on the balance between these two. Unlike most diet programs which limit one or the other, Paleo Diet recommends healthy amounts of both.

Better Cognitive Health

Fish are one of the best sources of protein in a Paleo Diet. Cold water fish such as salmon contains a lot of omega-3 fatty acids. This fatty acid is a great source of DHA which is good for the heart and eyes. It's an essential factor for better brain development too! Omega-3 can also be found on eggs and grass-fed meats!

Less Allergies

I know, allergies are very irritating. Fortunately, you will not experience such in a Paleo Diet. As we all know, most allergens come from grain and dairy products.

Other Benefits of Paleo Diet

- Lower risks of diabetes, cancer and heart disease

- Healthier skin and hair

- Better mood

- Better immunity against diseases

- Better insulin sensitivity and decreased insulin secretion (which consequently decreases fats)

- Reduced inflammations

- Stable energy levels

- No more calorie counting (yes, that's right!)

- And many, many more!

What Makes This Book Extra Special

At this point, I'm pretty sure you've gained enough understanding about Paleo Diet and its awesome health benefits. Since I want you to experience the best of paleo, all recipes in this book are adapted for slow cooking. Why? Below are some of its amazing benefits.

Very Delicious and Nutritious Meals

Fresh ingredients cooked for long periods of time at a low temperature retains the natural juices of meats and vegetables. These juices are not only delicious, they're packed with nutrients too!

A Time for Doing Things that You Love

Do you want to spend more time with your kids? Slow cooking does not require you to sit in front of a stove for hours. The only time-consuming part are the preparations. Once everything is set, you are free to do all the things you love while your slow cooker do its job.

Paleo Slow Cooker Recipes

Soups

Moroccan Soup with Lentils and Tomatoes

Ingredients:

2 cups diced red onions

2 cups diced carrots

4 garlic cloves, finely chopped

1-2 tsp extra-virgin olive oil

1/2-1 tsp cumin powder

1/2-1 tsp coriander powder

1/2-1 tsp turmeric powder

1/4 tsp cinnamon powder

1/4 tsp black pepper powder

6 cups chicken broth

2-3 cups water

3 cups sliced cauliflower florets

1 3/4-2 cups lentils

28 ounces diced tomatoes

1-2 tbsp tomato paste

4 cups sliced fresh spinach

1/2 cup sliced fresh cilantro

2 tbsp freshly squeezed lemon juice

Instructions:

1. In a slow cooker, place all ingredients except for spinach, cilantro and lemon juice.

2. Mix all ingredients until well combined and cover the pot with a lid.

3. Set on high heat and cook for 5 hours.

4. On the last 30 minutes of cooking, add sliced spinach.

5. Ladle soup in a bowl and top with sliced cilantro.

6. Drizzle soup with lemon juice and then serve.

Miso Soup with Peas and Carrots

Ingredients:

5 cups vegetable stock, low sodium

3-5 cups water

4 cups split peas, drained and rinsed

1 cup finely sliced carrots

2 garlic cloves, pressed and minced

1 large red onion, sliced

2-4 tbsp white miso paste

1-3 tbsp coconut oil

Pinch of sea salt and black pepper powder

Instructions:

1. In a slow cooker, combine all ingredients except for stock and water. Mix until well blended.

2. Pour stock and water into the pot and stir to combine.

3. Cover the pot with a lid and cook for 5-6 hours on high heat.

4. Ladle soup in a bowl and then serve.

Crab Meat in Creamy Sherry Sauce

Ingredients:

26 ounces fresh crab meat, flaked

28 ounces cream of mushroom

6 tbsp fresh butter

1/4-1/2 cup dry sherry

1/2-1 tsp Worcestershire sauce

1/2 cup cream, light

Pinch of sea salt and black pepper powder

3 green onions, diced

2 medium-sized eggs, lightly whisked

Instructions:

1. On a high heat setting slow cooker, combine all ingredients except for the eggs and cook for an hour.

2. Then turn the setting to low and continue cooking for 2-3 hours.

3. On the last hour of cooking, add the eggs and stir.

4. Place in a large bowl and serve.

Onion Soup

Ingredients:

3 large sweet onions, sliced thinly

3 cups beef broth, low sodium

3 cups chicken broth, low sodium

1-2 cups water

3 tbsp coconut or olive oil

1 1/2 tsp thyme leaves, dried

Pinch of sea salt and black pepper

Instructions:

1. Caramelize onions with oil in a slow cooker for 9-12 hours on high heat setting.

2. Add beef and chicken stock, thyme leaves, sea salt and black pepper.

3. Turn the switch to low heat setting and cook for 9 hours.

4. Ladle soup in a bowl and then serve.

Meaty Beet and Carrot Soup

Ingredients:

4 medium-sized, peeled beets, chopped

4 medium-sized peeled and chopped carrots

3 cups beef stock, low sodium

1/2 tsp Celtic sea salt

1/4 tsp black pepper, ground

1/4 tsp cayenne pepper, diced

1/4 cup dill, diced

2 garlic cloves, chopped

Instructions:

1. Set slow cooker on low heat and add beets, carrots and beef stock.

2. Cover pot with the lid and cook for 6-8 hours.

3. Add dill, pepper, salt and cloves and stir to combine.

4. Pour mixture into the blender and pulse until the texture is smooth.

5. Pour soup in a bowl and then serve.

Minestrone Soup

Ingredients:

2 tbsp extra-virgin olive oil

1 yellow sweet potato or yam, diced

1 cup diced carrots

2 fresh celery stalks, chopped

2 fresh zucchini squash, chopped

2 fresh shallots, chopped

2 garlic cloves, minced

28 ounces meat or vegetable broth

28 ounces diced tomatoes with juice

1/2 cup fresh spinach, chopped

2 bay leaves, dried

2 tsp oregano, dried

1 tsp basil leaves, fresh

1 tsp fresh parsley, chopped

1/4-1/2 tsp cayenne pepper

1/4 tsp Himalayan sea salt

1 1/2 pound cooked ground pork

Instructions:

1. In a slow cooker, drizzle the oil and add the rest of the ingredients except for the ground pork.

2. Mix all ingredients until well combined and cover pot with the lid.

3. Set the slow cooker to low and cook for 5-8 hours.

4. On the last 2 hours of cooking, add the cooked ground pork.

5. Discard the bay leaves and ladle soup into a bowl.Serve and enjoy while still hot.

Chicken Lemon Soup with Kale

Ingredients:

3-4 cups shredded chicken

6 cups bone broth or stock

1 small bunch of kale, sliced into strips

Zest of 3 medium-sized lemons

2 tbsp freshly squeezed lemon juice

1 cup chopped onions

1/2 cup extra-virgin olive oil

Pinch of salt

Instructions:

1. Place 2 cups of broth or stock, chopped onions and olive oil in a blender until the texture is smooth.

2. Pour mixture into a slow cooker and add 4 cups of broth, sliced kale, chicken, lemon zest and juice and salt.

3. Cook on low for 6 hours while stirring occasionally.

4. Ladle the soup into a bowl and serve while hot.

Sweet Potato Basil Soup

Ingredients:

2 sweet

diced

1/2-1 yellow onion, sliced

1 4 ounces coconut milk

1 cup vegetable broth

2 cloves of garlic, minced

1 tbsp basil

Pinch of salt and black pepper

Instructions:

1. Combine sweet potatoes, onions, coconut milk, broth, minced cloves, dried basil, sea salt and black pepper in a slow cooker and mix until well combined.

2. Cover the pot with the lid and cook on high for 3 hours.

3. Pour mixture into the blender and pulse until the texture is smooth.

4. Ladle soup into a bowl and serve.

Main Dish

Seafood

Salmon Fillet in Maple Sauce

Ingredients:

6 salmon fillets, regular size

1/2 cup maple syrup or agave syrup

1/8 cup lime juice, freshly squeezed

1/4 cup soy sauce, wheat-free

2 tsp minced garlic

1 tsp crushed ginger root

Instructions:

1. In a bowl, stir syrup, juice, soy sauce, garlic and ginger root until well blended.

2. On the bottom of the slow cooker, place the salmon and pour in the liquid mixture.

3. Cover the pot with the lid and cook for an hour on high heat setting.

Zesty Lime Salmon with Cilantro

Ingredients:

3-4 salmon fillets

3/4 cup chopped fresh cilantro

2 garlic cloves, pressed and minced

2-3 tbsp lime juice, freshly squeezed

1 tbsp extra-virgin olive oil

1/4 tsp sea salt

Instructions:

1. In a greased slow cooker, place the salmon fillets and set aside.

2. In a bowl, mix fresh cilantro, cloves, juice, olive oil and salt.

3. Add mixture over the fillets and cover the pot with the lid.

4. Set the pot on high heat and cook for 1-2 hours.

5. Place on a plate and then serve.

Creamy Salmon Flakes with Sweet Potatoes

Ingredients:

5 medium-sized peeled and sliced sweet potatoes

3 tbsp all-purpose flour

1/8 tsp Celtic sea salt

1/8 tsp ground black pepper

16 ounces drained salmon, flaked

1/2 cup chopped red or yellow onion

10 3/4 ounces cream of mushroom

1/4-1/2 cup water

Pinch of ground nutmeg

Instructions:

1. Combine half of the sweet potatoes, 1 1/2 tbsp flour, salt and pepper into a slow cooker.

2. Top the mixture with 8 ounces salmon flakes and half of the chopped onions.

3. Repeat the layers with the remaining ingredients.

4. Pour water/cream soup mixture and drizzle with nutmeg powder.

5. Cover the pot with the lid and cook for 8-9 hours on low heat setting.

6. Place on a plate and serve.

Bacon-wrapped Eel in Red Wine Sauce

Ingredients:

8 pieces 3-4 inch-sized eels

8 pieces bacon strips

2 tbsp lemon juice, freshly squeezed

2 tbsp vegetable oil or olive oil

1 cup red wine

1 large red onion, chopped

2 tbsp chopped fresh parsley

1 tsp dried sage leaves

1-2 egg yolk

2 tbsp heavy cream

Instructions:

1. Combine lemon juice, oil, wine, parsley an onion in a bowl.

2. Place eels on a dish and pour mixture and set aside.

3. Sprinkle each eel with sage and wrap with bacon strip.

4. In a slow cooker, place wrapped eels neatly and pour marinade liquid.

5. Set pot in low heat and cook for 6 hours.

6. Place cooked eels on a plate and set aside.

7. Mix the heavy cream with the egg yolk and stir into the pot.

8. Place the cooked eels back into the pot and cook for another 15 minutes.

9. Place on a plate and serve.

Tilapia Fillet with Lemon Mayo Sauce

Ingredients:

2-4 Tilapia fillets or any white fish of your choice

5 tbsp lemon juice, freshly squeezed

4 garlic cloves, pressed and minced

1/8 tsp Himalayan sea salt

1/8 tsp freshly ground black pepper

Instructions:

1. In a bowl, mix juice, cloves, salt and pepper until well blended.

2. Pour mixture on each fillet and wrap with foil.

3. Stack foiled fillets into a slow cooker and cover with the lid.

4. Set the pot on low heat and cook for 3-4 hours.

Citrus Fish

Ingredients:

1 1/2 pounds fish fillets, any kind of fish

1/8 tsp Celtic sea salt

1/8 tsp black pepper powder

1/2 cup diced red onion

5 tbsp sliced fresh parsley

1 tbsp vegetable or olive oil

2 tsp freshly grated lemon rind

2 tsp freshly grated orange rind

3-4 slices, orange and lemon

Instructions:

1. Grease slow cooker with olive oil and place fish fillet with salt and pepper into the cooker.

2. Cover the pot with the lid and cook for 1-2 hours on low heat setting.

3. Place the cooked fish on a plate.

4. Top cooked fish with orange and lemon slices and then serve.

Spicy Shrimp Stew

Ingredients:

1 pound fresh, shelled and deveined shrimp

1 1/2-2 cups diced celery

1 1/4 cups diced red onion

3/4 cups diced green or red bell pepper

8 ounces tomato sauce

28 ounces whole tomatoes

1 garlic clove, pressed and minced

1 tsp sea salt

1/4 tsp ground black pepper

1/4-1/2 tsp hot sauce

Instructions:

1. In a slow cooker, place celery, onions, bell peppers, tomato sauce, whole tomatoes, clove, salt, black pepper and hot sauce.

2. Cover the pot with the lid and cook on high heat for 3-4 hours.

3. On the last hour of cooking, add fresh shrimps.

4. Place in a bowl and serve.

Spicy Jambalaya with Cajun

Ingredients:

1 pound large-sized shrimps, raw and deveined

1 pound chicken, cubed

5 cups beef stock or chicken stock

4 green or red bell peppers, chopped

1 large –sized red onion, chopped

2 cloves of garlic, diced

1 28 ounces diced tomatoes

4 bay leaves, dried

2-3 tbsp Cajun seasoning

1/4-1/2 cup red, hot sauce

1 head of cauliflower, cut into florets

2 cups fresh okra

1/2 tsp chopped thyme

2 tsp chopped parsley

2 celery ribs, chopped

2 tsp oregano, dried

Instructions:

1. Combine beef stock, red bell peppers, onion, garlic, canned diced tomatoes , bay leaves, chicken, hot

sauce, chopped thyme, parsley, celery and oregano in a slow cooker.

2. Cover and cook for 6 hours on low setting.

3. Meanwhile, place cauliflower in a food processor and process until texture is grainy.

4. Put processed cauliflower into the slow cooker, and add the raw shrimps and okra.

5. Continue cooking until vegetables are tender and shrimps are cook.

6. Place on a plate and serve.

Beef

Beef Stew

Ingredients:

2 pounds organic beef

2 cups stock, chicken or beef

1/2-1 tbsp balsamic vinegar

1 medium-sized red onion, chopped

2 celery stalks, coarsely chopped

2 large, peeled carrots, chopped

1-3 minced garlic cloves

1/2-1 tbsp paprika

3 dried bay leaves

1/2 tsp sea salt

1/2 tsp ground black pepper

1 tsp dried rosemary

1 tsp dried basil

1 tsp dried oregano

Instructions:

1. In a slow cooker, place beef together with the stock and vinegar.

2. Add the remaining ingredients and then cover the pot with the lid.

3. Cook for 7-8 hours on low setting.

4. Ladle in a large bowl and then serve.

Beef Strips in Mongolian Sauce

Ingredients:

1 1/2 pounds beef steak or any meat, sliced into thin strips

2 tbsp extra-virgin olive oil

1/2 tsp freshly diced ginger

2 garlic cloves, minced

3/4 cup wheat-free soy sauce

3/4-1 cup water

3/4 cup sugar, brown or white

1/4 cup non-GMO cornstarch

1/2 cup carrots, shredded

3 medium-sized green onions, chopped

Instructions:

1. Combine all ingredients except for the steak and the cornstarch in a slow cooker and mix until well blended.

2. Coat each piece of steak with cornstarch and place in the slow cooker.

3. Cook on high heat setting for 3 hours or on low heat setting for 5 hours.

4. Place steak on a plate and serve with steamed vegetables.

Roast Beef in Coffee Sauce

Ingredients:

2-3 pounds beef or pork roast

5 garlic cloves, pressed and halved

2 cups coffee, freshly brewed

Pinch of sea salt and black pepper

1 red onion, sliced

8 ounces mushrooms, halved

Instructions:

1. Cut slits on the roast and fill each slit with sliced cloves.

2. Coat the roast with salt and pepper.

3. In a slow cooker, lay first the roast and then add mushrooms, onions and brewed coffee.

4. Cover the pot with the lid and cook for 7-8 hours on low heat setting.

Beef Broccoli

Ingredients:

1 pound beef, thinly sliced

1/4 cup soy sauce, wheat-free

1-2 tbsp white wine

1-2 tbsp vinegar, apple cider

1/2-1 tbsp brown sugar

1-2 tsp sesame oil

2 peeled garlic cloves, chopped

1/2 tsp red pepper flakes, ground

4-5 broccoli heads, cut into florets

Instructions:

1. In a slow cooker, place soy sauce, wine, vinegar, sesame oil, sugar and cloves and stir until well combined.

2. Add beef strips and mix until well coated.

3. Cover pot with the lid and cook for 8 hours on low heat setting.

4. Add broccoli florets at the last hour before cooking is done.

5. Place on a plate and serve.

Beef Heart with Carrots in Red Wine Sauce

Ingredients:

1 organic beef heart

3 peeled, red onions, sliced in half

6 peeled carrots, halved

10 garlic cloves, pressed and chopped

1 cup red wine or meat broth

Pinch of sea salt and black pepper

Instructions:

1. In a slow cooker, place onions, carrots and cloves.

2. Top vegetables with beef heart.

3. Add red wine, salt and pepper and cover pot with the lid.

4. Set pot on low heat setting and cook for 5-8 hours.

5. Place cooked beef heart on a chopping board and slice into strips.

6. Place strips on a plate and add vegetables on the side.

7. Serve and enjoy!

Seasoned Pot Roast with Green Chilies

Ingredients:

2-3 pounds pot roast of your choice

1 yellow or red onion, quartered

3-4 peeled garlic cloves, minced

7 ounces green chilies

1/3 cup lime juice, freshly squeezed

1/2-1 cup water

1 tbsp cumin powder

1 tsp oregano powder

Pinch of sea salt

Instructions:

1. In a slow cooker, combine all ingredients except for the roast and mix until well blended.

2. Add roast and cook for 5-8 hours on low heat setting.

3. Place on a plate and then serve.

Roast Beef in Pepper Sauce

Ingredients:

1 sirloin tip roast or any kind of roast

1 1/2 cups beef broth, low sodium

1/4 cup tamari sauce, organic

1 red pepper, chopped

1 green pepper, chopped

2 small red onions, chopped

1/8 tsp freshly ground black pepper

1 garlic clove, pressed

Instructions:

1. In a slow cooker, place roast and add the rest of the ingredients.

2. Cover the pot with the lid and cook under high setting for 3-4 hours.

3. Then place on a plate and serve.

Steak in Mushroom Gravy

Ingredients:

2 round steaks of your choice

1 1/2 cups beef broth

4 ounces mushrooms, chopped

1 garlic clove, minced

1 tsp Himalayan sea salt

1-2 tbsp arrowroot powder or (cornstarch)

1-2 tbsp water

Pinch of ground black pepper

Instructions:

1. In the slow cooker, place the steaks, broth, garlic, salt and pepper and cook on low setting for 8 hours.

2. Add the mushrooms on the last hour of cooking.

3. Place steaks on a plate and set aside.

4. Make a mixture of water and arrowroot powder.

5. Pour the mixture into the slow cooker and stir to combine.

6. Cook the mixture for a few minutes until it has thickened.

7. Drizzle gravy over the cooked steak and serve.

Corned Beef and Cabbage

Ingredients:

2 pounds corned beef brisket, lean

1 cup chopped onions

2 medium-sized peeled carrots, sliced into 1-inch thick

2 medium-sized peeled and chopped parsnips

6 cabbage wedges

1/4 cup diced fresh parsley

2 bay leaves, dried

1/8 tsp whole peppercorns, cracked

3 cups water

Instructions:

1. Combine all ingredients except for the cabbage in the slow cooker.

2. Cover the pot and cook for 3-4 hours on high heat setting.

3. Place the cabbage and continue cooking for 1 1/2 hours.

4. Cut the meat into desired thickness and place on the plate.

5. Serve with rice or steamed vegetables and enjoy.

Beef and Eggplant Stew

Ingredients:

1 pound cooked ground beef or lamb

1 red or green bell pepper, chopped

1 large-sized eggplant, cubed

1 large-sized sweet onion, peeled and chopped

10 peeled garlic cloves, chopped

1-2 tbsp ground cumin

3-4 tbsp sweet paprika

1-2 tsp ground cinnamon

1-2 tsp sea salt

4-5 tbsp tomato paste

Water, to cover all ingredients

1-2 tbsp parsley, freshly chopped

Instructions:

1. In slow cooker filled with simmering water, place beef, bell pepper, eggplant, onion, cloves, cumin, paprika, cinnamon, salt and tomato paste and water.

2. Mix the ingredients until well combined and cover with the lid.

3. On a low setting, cook the mixture for 10-12 hours while stirring occasionally.

4. Ladle soup into serving bowls and top with chopped parsley.

Meatloaf with Worcestershire Sauce

Ingredients:

2 pounds of ground meat, beef (or turkey)

1 medium-sized red onion, finely chopped

2-3 tbsp Worcestershire sauce

1/2-1 tsp garlic salt

Pinch of sea salt and black pepper powder

2 medium-sized eggs, whisked

Instructions:

1. In a large bowl, combine all ingredients and mix until well blended.

2. Pour mixture into the slow cooker and cover with the lid.

3. Cook for 3-4 hours on high heat setting.

4. Let it cool for a few minutes and slice on the desired thickness.

5. Place on a plate and serve.

Lamb

Herbed Lamb Roast

Ingredients:

2 1/2-3 pounds lamb roast

10 peeled garlic cloves, crushed

10-15 kalamata olives, pitted

3-4 tbsp olive juice

1/2-1 tbsp fresh rosemary

1/2-1 tbsp fresh thyme

Pinch of sea salt and black pepper

1-2 cups water

Instructions:

1. In a slow cooker, place the lamb roast and add cloves, olives, olive juice, salt and pepper.

2. Add water, rosemary and thyme and cover pot with the lid.

3. Set pot on low setting and cook for 6-8 hours.

4. Place roast on a plate and then serve.

Herbed Lamb Shanks with Carrots

Ingredients:

2 organic lamb shanks

1 leek, chopped

3 carrots, coarsely chopped

3 sprigs of thyme, freshly chopped

3 garlic cloves, finely chopped

1-2 cups water

Pinch of Celtic sea salt and ground black pepper

Instructions:

1. Place lamb shank into the slow cooker with water and sprinkle salt and black pepper.

2. Add leeks, carrots, garlic and thyme and cover with the lid.

3. Cook for 6 hours on high setting.

4. Place in a large bowl and serve while hot.

Lamb Shank Curry with Pumpkin

Ingredients:

4 pieces lamb shanks

1 pound pumpkin, sliced

1/2 cup diced dates

1 red or yellow onion, diced

4 garlic cloves, diced

1/2 pound coconut cream

4-6 cups water

3 bay leaves, dried

1 tbsp ginger, ground

1 tsp black pepper powder

1 tbsp paprika powder

1 tbsp cumin powder

1 tbsp turmeric powder

1 tsp pressed and minced chili

1 tsp cinnamon powder

1/8 tsp salt

Instructions:

1. In a slow cooker, dump onion, cloves, dried bay leaves, ginger, pepper, paprika, cumin, turmeric, chili,

cinnamon, salt, coconut cream, water and pieces of lamb shanks.

2. Cook for 2 hours on low heat setting.

3. Place sliced pumpkins and dates and continue cooking for 6 hours.

4. Discard bay leaves and meat bones.

5. Place in a bowl and then serve immediately.

Chicken

Chicken Wraps with Sour Cream

Ingredients:

1/2 cup chopped red or white onion

1 pound chicken thighs, boneless

1 1/2 tsp seasoning, lemon pepper

1 garlic clove, pressed and minced

1/4 tsp ground cinnamon

1/2 tsp ground oregano

1 tsp sea salt

4 pieces pita bread

1/2-1 cup sour cream

1/4 cup chopped tomato

Instructions:

1. In a greased slow cooker, place the chicken thighs at the bottom.

2. Top the chicken with onions, garlic cloves, cinnamon, oregano and salt.

3. Cover the slow cooker and cook for 7-8 hours on low heat setting.

4. Then place the cooked chicken on a plate and shred using a fork.

5. Add the sour cream and shredded chicken into the slow cooker.

6. Mix until chicken is well coated.

7. Place a spoonful of chicken mixture on each pieces of pita bread.

8. Roll pita breads and then serve.

Chicken Stew in Tomato Sauce

Ingredients:

2 pounds skinless chicken fillet

1 small red onion, diced

1 pressed garlic clove, minced

1 red bell pepper, chopped

4 plum tomatoes, fresh

2 tbsp pitted olives

8 ounces tomato sauce

1/4 tsp ground oregano

1/4 tsp ground cumin

Pinch of sea salt

1-2 bay leaf, dried

1/4 cup sliced cilantro

1/2 cup water

1 tbsp brine solution

Instructions:

1. In a slow cooker, combine chicken fillet, onion, garlic clove, pepper, plum tomatoes, salt, cumin and oregano and mix until well blended.

2. Add tomato sauce, olives, brine, water, bay leaf and cilantro and cover pot with the lid.

3. Set on high heat and cook for 3-4 hours.

4. Place on a plate and sprinkle with cilantro and serve.

Chicken Mushroom in Tomatillo Salsa

Ingredients:

6 chicken breast fillets

12 ounces tomatillo salsa

8 ounces mushrooms, halved

2 red bell peppers, halved

2 jalapeños, halved

1 red or yellow onion, sliced

1 tomato, quartered

2 garlic cloves, peeled and minced

1 tbsp lemon juice, freshly squeezed

1 tsp sea salt

1 tsp black pepper powder

1 tsp oregano powder

1 tsp cumin powder

Instructions:

1. In a slow cooker, lay chicken fillet on the bottom.

2. Combine bell pepper, onion, jalapeños, mushrooms, tomato, cloves, salsa, juice, salt, pepper, oregano and cumin and mix until well blended.

3. Pour mixture into the pot and cover with the lid.

4. Set the pot of low heat and cook for 6 hours.

5. Place in a plate and then serve.

Kung Pao Chicken

Ingredients:

1 pound chicken thigh fillet

2 tbsp all-purpose flour, gluten-free

1/4 tsp ground black pepper

1/4 tsp red pepper powder

1/2-1 tbsp rice vinegar

1/2-1 tbsp soy sauce

1/2-1 tbsp sesame oil

1/2-1 tsp brown sugar

1 tsp pressed and diced garlic

1 tbsp tomato paste, without spices

1 tsp Tabasco sauce or any hot sauce

1 tsp chopped nuts

1 tsp chopped leeks

Instructions:

1. Coat chicken with flour and black and red pepper and place in the slow cooker.

2. Mix rice vinegar, soy sauce, sesame oil, sugar, garlic, tomato paste and hot sauce in a bowl and pour into the slow cooker.

3. Cover the pot with the lid and cook for 2-4 hours on low heat setting.

4. Turn the heat setting to high while removing the lid and cook for 10-15 minutes.

5. Place on a plate and then serve.

Chicken with Broccoli

Ingredients:

2 pounds chicken thighs, boneless

1/4 cup coconut aminos or soy sauce

2 cups broccoli or kale

1 cup peeled and sliced carrots

1/2-1 cup raw cashews

1/2 cup cilantro, freshly sliced

1 tbsp coconut or olive oil

1-2 tbsp rice wine vinegar

1 tbsp brown sugar or raw honey

2 tbsp ketchup

1 tbsp crushed and minced garlic

1/2 tsp black pepper powder

1 tsp sea salt

1/4 tsp red pepper, flaked

2 tsp minced ginger

Instructions:

1. In a greased slow cooker, place the chicken thighs and set aside.

2. In a bowl, combine coconut aminos, vinegar, honey, minced garlic and ginger, ketchup, red pepper flakes, pepper and salt and mix until well blended.

3. Pour mixture into the pot and cover with the lid.

4. Set the pot to low heat and cook for 5- 8 hours.

5. On the last hour of cooking, add broccoli.

6. Place in a bowl and top cashews and cilantro before serving.

Chicken with Sweet Potatoes

Ingredients:

1 whole, dressed chicken

Pinch of sea salt and black pepper powder

4-5 medium-sized washed sweet potatoes

1/4-1/2 cup extra-virgin olive oil

Instructions:

1. Coat sweet potatoes with oil, salt and pepper and wrap with aluminum foil.

2. Place wrapped sweet potatoes in the slow cooker.

3. Place seasoned chicken over wrapped sweet potatoes and cover with the lid.

4. Set the pot on low heat and cook for 4-6 hours.

5. Place cooked chicken on a plate and place sweet potatoes at the side.

6. Serve and enjoy!

Peppered Chicken Cacciatore

Ingredients:

1 pound frozen skinless chicken fillet

3 tbsp extra-virgin olive oil

1 large-sized, seeded and chopped green pepper

1 large-sized, seeded and chopped red pepper

1 large-sized, seeded and chopped yellow pepper

1 large piece celery stalk, chopped

3 large, peeled garlic cloves, pressed and minced

1 4 1/2 ounces diced tomatoes

Instructions:

1. In a resealable bag, place all ingredients and tightly seal the bag.

2. Place bag in the freezer for an hour or overnight.

3. Before cooking, thaw the mixture and put it inside the slow cooker.

4. Cover pot with the lid and cook for 8 hours on low heat setting.

5. Serve and enjoy.

Zesty Lemon Chicken

Ingredients:

2-2 1/2 pounds chicken drumsticks

1/2 cup extra-virgin olive oil

1/2 cup chicken stock, low sodium

2 medium-sized lemons

1 red or yellow onion, sliced

2 peeled garlic cloves, crushed

1/2 tsp fresh rosemary

1/2 tsp fresh paprika

Pinch of sea salt and black pepper powder

Instructions:

1. In a resealable freezer bag, place all ingredients and squeeze the lemons for the juice and include the lemon peel in the bag.

2. Tightly seal the bag and place in the freezer overnight.

3. Thaw the mixture before cooking.

4. In a slow cooker, place all the contents of the bag and cook for 3-4 hours on high heat setting.

5. Place cooked chicken on a plate and serve.

Chicken Adobo

Ingredients:

8 chicken thighs, skinless

1/3 -1 cup coconut aminos or soy sauce

1/3-1 cup apple cider vinegar

1 peeled garlic clove, smashed

6 black peppercorns, freshly ground

4 bay leaves, dried

1 small-sized diced Jalapeño pepper

Instructions:

1. Make a marinade by mixing aminos, vinegar, garlic, chopped jalapeño and ground pepper.

2. Pour marinade in a plastic bag and add chicken.

3. Seal the bag and let it sit for an hour or a day.

4. In a slow cooker, place the chicken with marinade and add bay leaves.

5. Cover pot with the lid and set to low and cook for 7-8 hours or until chicken is tender.

6. Remove bay leaves and place chicken on a plate.

7. Serve with steamed rice or mixed vegetables.

Cheesy Chicken with Mangoes in Coconut Milk

Ingredients:

1 pound chicken breasts, sliced into cubes

1 can coconut milk, full fat

2 small-sized mangoes, peeled and cubed

1 tbsp dried flakes of chipotle

Instructions:

1. In the slow cooker, pour coconut milk and add mangoes, chicken and chipotle.

2. Stir mixture until well combined and then cover with the lid.

3. Cook the mixture for 3 hours on high setting.

4. Place on the plate and serve.

Chicken with Honey Soy Sauce

Ingredients:

2 pounds skinless chicken fillet

1/2 cup coconut aminos or soy sauce

1 tbsp raw honey

1 tbsp ginger, freshly grated

2 cloves of garlic, minced

1/8 tsp Celtic ea salt

1/8 tsp freshly ground black pepper

Instructions:

1. Combine coconut aminos, raw honey, grated ginger and minced garlic cloves until well blended and set aside.

2. In a slow cooker, place the chicken fillet and pour over the sauce.

3. Cover with the lid and cook for 5 hours on low setting.

4. Place the cooked chicken on a plate and set aside.

5. Season remaining liquid with salt and pepper.

6. Drizzle liquid mixture on top of the cooked chicken and serve.

Chicken with Belgian Endive in Apple Sauce

Ingredients:

2 pounds skinless chicken fillet

3 cored Belgian endive, sliced into strips

1 apple, sliced

1/2 cup apple juice

1-2 tbsp caraway seeds

1 tsp sea salt

Black pepper

Instructions:

1. In a slow cooker, place the chicken and add caraway seeds, sea salt and cracked black pepper.

2. Top chicken thighs with a layer of endives and apple slices.

3. Pour apple juice and cover the pot with the lid.

4. Cook on low setting for 6 hours.

5. Place on a plate and serve.

Cilantro Chicken

Ingredients:

4-6 chicken thighs, skinless

2 cups diced yellow onions

2 cups freshly chopped cilantro

1 cup coconut milk

2 tbsp minced garlic cloves

1 tbsp minced Serrano Chile pepper

1 tbsp fresh ginger, finely grated

1 tbsp olive oil

3/4 tsp freshly ground coriander

3/4 tsp sea salt

1/2 tsp freshly ground cumin

1/2 tsp freshly ground fenugreek

1/4 tsp black pepper, freshly ground

Instructions:

1. Place onion, garlic, Chile pepper, ginger, cilantro into the slow cooker.

2. Pour coconut milk and season with salt and black pepper.

3. Stir the mixture until well combined.

4. Add chicken into the mixture.

5. Cook on high for 3 hours or on low for 5 hours.

6. Serve with rice and enjoy!

Chicken in Red Curry Sauce

Ingredients:

1 1/2 pounds skinless chicken fillet, cut into cubes

1 cup chicken broth

2 cans coconut milk

2-3 tbsp red curry paste (Thai House)

1 small, diced yellow onion

1/2 medium-sized diced red bell pepper

1/2 medium-sized diced green bell pepper

1/4 cauliflower head, cut into florets

1/4 cabbage head, sliced into thin strips

3 pressed garlic cloves, minced

Instructions:

1. In a slow cooker, place coconut milk, chicken broth and curry paste and stir until curry paste dissolves.

2. Add chicken meat cubes, onions, red and green bell pepper, cauliflower, cabbage and garlic into the pot and stir.

3. Cover the pot with the lid and cook for 4 hours on low heat setting.

4. Place chicken curry in a bowl and serve.

Sweet Chicken Fillet with Dijon Mustard

Ingredients:

6 chicken breasts, fillet

1/4 cup raw honey

1/4-1/2 cup Dijon mustard

1/2 cup chicken broth, low sodium

Instructions:

1. In a bowl, combine raw honey, mustard and broth until well blended.

2. Dip each chicken breast in the mixture until well coated and place neatly in the slow cooker.

3. Pour remaining mixture in the pot and cover with the lid.

4. Cook for 3 hours on high heat and continue to cook for another 3 hours on low heat.

5. Place cooked chicken on a plate and serve.

Chicken with Cabbage Kimchi

Ingredients:

1 cup chicken broth

4 chopped scallions, green part

6 minced garlic cloves

1-2 tbsp soy sauce

1-2 tsp palm sugar

1-2 tbsp dark sesame oil

1 tsp freshly grated ginger

2 pounds skinless chicken fillet

2 cups drained cabbage kimchi

Instructions:

1. In the slow cooker, place chicken broth, soy sauce, sugar, sesame oil and ginger and mix until well combined.

2. Add chicken thighs and combine with sauce until well coated.

3. Cover with the lid and cook for 4 hours on low heat setting.

4. Add kimchi and cook for 20 more minutes.

5. Place on the plate and garnish with chopped scallions.

6. Serve and enjoy.

Sweet Chicken Wings

Ingredients:

20-30 pieces chicken wings

3/4 cup honey

1 1/2 tbsp garlic, minced

2 tbsp extra-virgin olive oil

1/2 tsp Himalayan sea salt

1/2 tsp black pepper, freshly ground

Instructions:

1. Fill the slow cooker with chicken wings and set aside.

2. Combine honey, garlic, olive oil salt and pepper in a small bowl until well blended.

3. Pour mixture over the chicken wings and cover with the lid.

4. Cook on high for 3-4 hours or on low for 5-6 hours.

5. Place cooked chicken wings on a plate and serve.

Pork

Herbed Pork Roast with Dijon Mustard

Ingredients:

2-3 pounds pork

4 tbsp Dijon mustard

4 tbsp extra-virgin olive oil

1 1/2 tbsp coconut aminos or wheat-free soy sauce

1 tbsp oregano

1 tsp dried tarragon

1 tsp dried basil

Instructions:

1. In a bowl, combine mustard, olive oil, coconut, oregano, tarragon and basil and mix until well blended.

2. Place pork into the slow cooker and pour mixture over it.

3. Cover pot with the lid and cook for 10 hours on low.

4. Serve with mixed vegetables and enjoy!

Short Ribs in Korean BBQ Sauce

Ingredients:

3 pounds short ribs or oxtail

1/3-1 cup wheat-free soy sauce

1/3-1 cup fish sauce

5-6 tbsp apple cider vinegar

2 tbsp sesame oil, cold pressed

1/2-1 tsp red pepper flakes

5 garlic cloves, minced

1 tsp ground ginger

1/2 cup melted raw honey

1 medium-sized red onion, quartered

1 medium-sized carrot, cubed

1/2 cup beef stock, low-sodium

Instructions:

1. In a bowl, combine soy sauce, fish sauce, minced garlic, ground ginger, red pepper flakes, raw honey and vinegar until well blended and set aside.

2. In the slow cooker, place the onions, carrots, ribs and oxtail.

3. Pour the liquid mixture into the cooker and then add the broth.

4. Cover with the lid and cook for 7-8 hours on high setting.

5. Place on the plate and serve.

Tender Pork with Apples in Maple Orange Sauce

Ingredients:

2 1/2-3 pounds pork shoulder, sliced into chunks

1 tsp Celtic sea salt

1/2 tsp ground black pepper

1/2 tsp sage, dried

1/2 cup orange juice, freshly squeezed

1 tbsp maple syrup or agave syrup

1 cored apple, peeled and chopped

Instructions:

1. Coat with salt, pepper and sage each pork chunks.

2. Place in the slow cooker and add chopped apples, orange juice and maple syrup.

3. Cover with the lid and cook under low setting for 5-6 hours.

4. Shred cooked pork using a fork and place on a plate.

5. Serve with steamed vegetables.

Honey Pork Lettuce Wraps

Ingredients:

2-3 pounds pork shoulder or any pork roast

Pinch of salt and black pepper

3-4 whole garlic cloves, smashed

3-4 tbsp wheat-free soy sauce

1-2 tbsp smooth almond or peanut butter

1 tbsp melted raw honey

1-2 tbsp vinegar

1-2 tsp sesame oil

1/2-1 tbsp Sriracha

1/2 tsp ground black pepper

1 tbsp ginger, minced

1 head of lettuce

1 tsp chopped cilantro

Instructions:

1. Place meat into the slow cooker and set aside.

2. In a bowl, combine coconut aminos, almond butter, honey, vinegar, sesame oil, sriracha, ground black pepper and minced ginger and mix until well blended.

3. Pour mixture over the meat and cook on low setting for 5-6 hours.

4. Shred the meat using a fork and place on top of the lettuce.

5. Roll or fold lettuce leaves and place on a plate.

6. Garnish with chopped cilantro and serve.

Pulled Pork with Pineapples

Ingredients:

3-4 pounds pork shoulder

1 can cubed pineapples in water

2 tbsp freshly grated ginger

Instructions:

1. In a slow cooker, place pork shoulder and add pineapples with the liquid and ginger.

2. Cover the pot with the lid and cook for 6-8 hours on low heat setting.

3. Shred pork with a fork and place on a plate with the pineapples, and then serve.

Honey Apple Pork Tenderloin

Ingredients:

4 organic apples, cored and sliced

2 pounds pork tenderloin

2-3 tbsp. ground nutmeg

2 tbsp. honey

Instructions:

1. In the bottom of the slow cooker, spread sliced apples and sprinkle ground nutmeg.

2. Place pork tenderloin on top of the apple layer.

3. Place another layer of apples on top of the tenderloin and sprinkle with ground nutmeg

4. Cook on low heat for 4-5 hours or until tenderloin is golden brown and tender.

5. Serve and enjoy.

Pork Loin in Butternut Squash Stew

Ingredients:

2 1/2 pounds cubed pork loin

4 cups peeled butternut squash, sliced into 1-inch thick

1 cup chicken broth, low sodium

1/4 cup coconut milk, full fat

2-3 leeks, trimmed and sliced

3-4 celery stalks, chopped

1-2 shallots, diced

6-10 cloves of garlic, thinly sliced

1-2 tsp garam masala

1-2 tsp sea salt

1-2 tsp lemon juice, freshly squeezed

Instructions:

1. Place all ingredients in a slow cooker and mix until well combined.

2. Cook the mixture on either high for 5 hours or low for 7 hours.

3. Ladle stew into bowls and serve.

Vegetable

Garlic Mashed Cauliflower

Ingredients:

1 cauliflower head, cut into florets

2-3 cups water

4 large, peeled garlic cloves

1 tsp Celtic sea salt

1 bay leaf, dried

1 tbsp organic butter

Pinch of sea salt and black pepper powder

Instructions:

1. In a slow cooker, place the florets, water, cloves, salt and pepper.

2. Cover the pot with the lid and cook on high heat setting for 2-3 hours.

3. Discard the liquid, bay leaf and cloves.

4. Add butter mix until the butter melts.

5. Place cooked cauliflower in a blender and pulse until smooth and creamy.

6. Place on a plate and season with salt and pepper.

7. Serve and enjoy!

Cannellini Beans with Sage

Ingredients:

1 pound cannellini beans, drained and rinsed

6 garlic cloves, pressed and minced

1 sprig fresh sage, chopped

1/8 tsp Celtic sea salt

1/8 tsp ground black pepper

8 cups water

6 tsp extra-virgin olive oil

Instructions:

1. In a slow cooker, place beans, cloves, salt and water.

2. Cover the pot with the lid and cook for 3 - 3 1/2 hours on high heat setting.

3. Discard liquid, clove and sage leaves.

4. Place beans in a bowl and drizzle with salt, pepper and olive oil.

5. Serve and enjoy!

Sweet Potato Quittata with Coconut Milk

Ingredients:

12 medium-sized eggs

2 cups diced sweet potato

1 cup coconut milk

1/2 pounds ham or any meat

1/2 cup chopped red onion

1/2 tsp Himalayan sea salt

1/4 tsp black pepper, freshly ground

Instructions:

1. Mix eggs, coconut milk, sea salt and black pepper until well combined.

2. In a slow cooker, pour the egg mixture and sprinkle ham and onion.

3. Cover the cooker with the lid and cook for 2-3 hours on high.

4. Let it cool and slice into squares and serve.

Desserts

Banana Loaf

Ingredients:

3 medium-sized bananas, ripe

1/4 cup softened butter

2 medium-sized eggs

1 tsp pure vanilla

1/4 cup sweetener of your choice

1 cup almond flour

1/2-1 tsp baking soda

Instructions:

1. In a bowl, place all ingredients and mix until well blended.

2. Pour mixture into a steel bowl and place bowl into the slow cooker.

3. Place layers of paper towels on top of the bowl and cover with the lid.

4. Cook for 2-3 hours on high heat setting.

5. Let it cool and slice to the desired thickness and then serve.

Cinnamon Apple Bread Pudding

Ingredients:

3 cored apples, peeled and cubed

2 cups almond or walnut flour

1/4 cup maple syrup or raw honey

2 medium-sized eggs

1 tbsp cinnamon powder

2 tsp baking powder, gluten-free

1/4-1/2 tsp baking soda

1 tsp vanilla, pure extract

1/8 tsp coconut or olive oil

Instructions:

1. In a large bowl, combine almond flour, cinnamon powder, gluten-free baking powder and baking soda.

2. Add cubed apples and mix until well coated and set aside.

3. In a small bowl, mix eggs, vanilla and syrup.

4. Pour mixture into the apple mixture and stir to combine.

5. Place into the greased slow cooker and cook for 5 hours on low heat setting.

6. Place on a plate and serve.

Honey Glazed Banana Foster

Ingredients:

4 medium-sized bananas

1-2 tbsp coconut oil

1-2 tbsp lemon juice

3 tbsp honey

1/4 tsp ground cinnamon

1/8 tsp ground nutmeg

1/8 tsp cloves

Instructions:

1. Cut bananas with 1/4-inch thickness and set aside.

2. In a high heated slow cooker, place coconut oil, lemon juice, honey, cinnamon, nutmeg and cloves.

3. Mix all ingredients until well combined and then reduce to low heat.

4. Add the sliced bananas and stir.

5. Cook for 1-2 hours on low.

6. Place bananas with honey mixture on a plate.

Sweet Apple Cinnamon Jam

Ingredients:

4 pounds cored apples, peeled and chopped

1/2-1 cup apple cider

1 tbsp cinnamon powder

1/2 tsp sea salt

1/4 tsp garlic clove

Instructions:

1. In a slow cooker, combine all ingredients and cook on high heat for 2 hours.

2. Then reduce to medium-low and cook for 14 hours.

3. Place apple butter on a clean jar for storage.

Part 2

Introduction

Clean and healthy food is important for your body because toxic junk and processed food are not good for your body. Paleo diet proves helpful for you to improve your health and reduce weight. Paleo diet is a healthy approach for you to stay strong, energetic and lean. You have to include healthy fats, fresh fruits and vegetables in your diet. Paleo Slow Cooker Meals will be a healthy addition to your diet. Modern diet consists of sugar, trans fats and processed foods. These unhealthy food items can increase the chances of obesity, heart disease, cancer, Parkinson's Alzheimer, diabetes, infertility and depression. If you want to build your healthy eating habits, you should include the followings in your regular routine:

Lean Protein

Lean protein means fish and chicken and other lean sources of protein. This protein proves helpful to support optimal immune function, healthy bones and strong muscle. After consuming protein, you will feel satisfied for a longer period of time.

Vegetables and Fruits

Fresh vegetables and fruits are rich in vitamins, antioxidants, phytonutrients and minerals. It will help you to decrease the chances of cancer, neurological decline and diabetes.

Healthy Fats

You should include seeds, nuts, olive oil, avocados, grass-fed meat and fish oil to get healthy food. These types of food items are rich with Omega-3 and Monounsaturated fats to decrease the probability of heart diseases, diabetes, obesity, cognitive decline and heart disease.

If you are following Paleo diet, you are allowed to eat vegetables, fruits, seafood, lean meats, seeds and nuts, healthy fats, etc. You should avoid grains, legumes, starches, processed food and sugar and alcohol.

While following Paleo diet, it can be difficult for you to decide your regular meals. There is no need to worry because this book has everything for your guidance. This book offers 25 healthy vegetarian and Paleo Chicken Recipes. To make your work easy, each recipe is available with complete details. You can use your slow cooker to make healthy meals for you and your family.

This Paleo Slow Cooker Cookbook has lots of delicious meat and vegetable recipes for you to discover. Get ready to save your time and prepare healthy meals without additional efforts. All recipes are designed for slow cooker to save your time and energy; hence, a working woman can easily follow a Paleo lifestyle and enjoy lots of health benefits.

Chapter 1 – Paleo Breakfast Recipes in
Slow Cooker

Start your day with a delicious Paleo breakfast that is easy to prepare in the slow cooker. It will save your time because you can start preparations for the night to get your breakfast ready in the morning.

Paleo Breakfast Pie

This pie has healthy ingredients for your breakfast. You can kick start your day with a good breakfast.

Cooking Time: 8 hours 10 minutes

Servings: 4 to 6

Ingredients:

- Whisked Eggs: 8
- Shredded sweet potato: 1
- Chicken Sausage (broken up): 1 lb.
- Diced onion: 1
- Garlic powder: 1 tablespoon
- Dried basil: 2 teaspoons
- Pepper and salt: As per taste
- Extra vegetables as per your choice: Optional

Cooking Instructions:

Grease your slow cooker with olive or coconut oil to avoid any sticking. Shred sweet potato with one shredder and wash these potatoes before adding them to your slow cooker.

Add all your ingredients in the slow cooker and use one spatula to mix everything well. Set your slow cooker on low setting for 6 to 8 hours and make slices of pie before serving it.

Casserole in Slow Cooker

Enjoy casserole with ground sausage, potatoes and kale. This casserole will be a good choice for your breakfast.

Cooking Time: 6 hours 15 Minutes

Servings: 6 Servings

Ingredients:

- Coconut Oil: 2 tablespoons
- Sliced Leek: 1 1/3 cups
- Chopped Kale: 1 cup
- Eggs: 8
- Sweet Potato (peeled and grated): 2/3 cups
- Beef Sausage: 1 ½ cups

Cooking Instructions:

Take one skillet and melt coconut oil and add garlic, kale and leeks. You have to sauté them for a few minutes. Take one large bowl and combine sautéed vegetables and remaining ingredients. Combine these ingredients in your slow cooker and cook on low setting for almost 4 – 6 hours.

Let it cool down and cut into slices to serve.

Low-carb Casserole

This healthy casserole will energize your body and keep your stomach full for a longer time. You can set its ingredients in slow cooker in the night.

Cooking Time: 6 to 8 hours

Servings: 4 to 6

Ingredients:

- Coconut Oil to Grease slow cooker
- Breakfast sausage (crumbled): 1/2 pound
- Chopped bacon: 6 ounces
- Diced yellow onion: 1/2 cup
- Sweet potatoes (remove skin and shredded): 1 pound
- Bell pepper (remove seeds and diced): 1 red
- Bell pepper (remove seeds and diced): 1 Orange
- Beaten eggs: 16
- Almond milk: 1/2 cup
- Coconut milk (full-fat): 1/4 cup
- Sea salt: 1 teaspoon

- Dry mustard: 3/4 teaspoon
- Black pepper (ground): 1/4 teaspoon
- Garnishing: Green onions

Cooking Instructions:

Grease one slow cooker with coconut oil and keep it aside.

Take a skillet and cook bacon, onion and sausage in this skillet on medium heat for almost 12 minutes. Drain off extra fat and keep it aside.

Add shredded potatoes in your slow cooker and press them slightly in the downward direction. It is time to add onion mixture, bell peppers and meat over shredded potatoes (in your slow cooker).

Take a bowl and whisk milk, salt, pepper, eggs and mustard. Pour this mixture into your slow cooker and cover this cooker to set on low setting for almost 6 – 8 hours. Once it is done, cut into slices and serve with the breakfast.

Cabbage and Apple Treat

You can start your day with apple and cabbage treat that is healthy to eat and easy to cook in your slow cooker.

Cooking Time: 6 to 8 hours

Servings: 6 to 8

Ingredients:

- Tart apples (diced): 2
- Chopped cabbage: 1 Medium
- Onion (Sliced): 1 large
- Salt: 1/2 teaspoon
- Ground pepper: 1/8 teaspoon
- Chicken stock: 1/2 cup
- Apple juice: 1 cup
- Spicy mustard: 3 tablespoons
- Coconut oil or Butter to Grease Inside Area of Crock Pot

Cooking Instructions:

Grease your slow cooker with coconut oil.

Add cabbage, apples and onions in the slow cooker along with pepper and salt. Mix these ingredients together.

Take one measuring cup and mix apple juice, mustard and chicken broth to combine them well. Pour this mixture over the ingredients in your slow cooker.

Cover this cooker and set on low heat for almost 6 – 8 hours. You can stir after every three hours.

Take out finished food in serving bowl and serve in breakfast.

Cinnamon Pancake

If you like some healthy pancakes in your breakfast, you can try this healthy and delicious recipe.

Cooking Time: 1 hour 35 minutes

Servings: 4

Ingredients:

- Bisquick Mix: 2 cups
- Milk: 1 cup
- Eggs: 2
- Vanilla: 1 teaspoon
- Granulated Sugar: 3 tablespoons
- Cinnamon Powder: 1 teaspoon
- Non-stick Spray

Cooking Instructions:

Take one large bowl to mix eggs, vanilla, milk, and Bisquick to make a smooth mixture. Grease your slow cooker with non-stick spray and pour Bisquick mixture in this cooker.

Take one separate bowl and mix cinnamon and sugar together. Mix these ingredients well and sprinkle this mixture equally over batter in slow cooker.

Use end of a spoon or butter knife to swirl the sugar and cinnamon in the batter to make beautiful swirls. Cook on high setting for almost 1 to 1 ½ hours to set pancake. Serve with your favorite Syrup.

Chapter 2– Paleo Starters and Snacks

You can prepare some delicious snacks and starters in the slow cooker to enhance the taste of your meals. These snacks are healthy and delicious at the same time.

Applesauce Chicken

You can prepare this sweet and savory chicken for your family. It is free from gluten and healthy for everyone.

Cooking Time: 7 hours

Servings: 4

Ingredients:

- Chicken (cleaned and trimmed): 2lbs or 4 breasts
- Organic Applesauce (unsweetened): 2 Cups
- Onion Powder: 1/2 Teaspoon
- Garlic Powder: 1/2 Teaspoon
- Black Pepper: 1/4 Teaspoon
- Cinnamon: 1/4 Teaspoon

Cooking Instructions:

Grease your slow cooker and add all ingredients in it. Cover this cooker and cook chicken for almost 7 hours on low setting. You can serve chicken with your favorite sauce.

Chicken Tacos

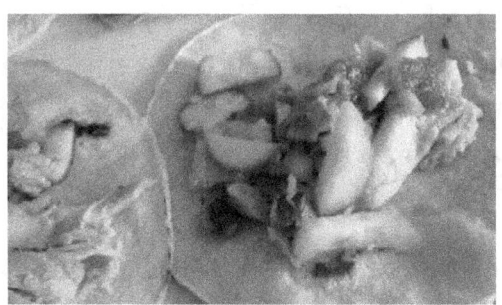

This special and spicy chicken is perfect to enjoy with lettuce wraps and other vegetables. It will keep you full and improve your health.

Cooking Time: 6 hours 10 minutes

Servings: 2

Ingredients:

- Chicken: 2 breasts
- Fresh tomatoes: 2
- Red onions: 2
- Garlic cloves: 2
- Honey: 1 tablespoon
- Basil: 1 teaspoon
- Chili powder: 1 teaspoon
- Whole cloves: 1 teaspoon
- Water: 3 tablespoons
- Lettuce leaves, red cabbage and Carrots

Cooking Instructions:

Cut tomatoes and onions into small chunks and finely chop garlic cloves.

Put chicken breasts in slow cooker and add all other ingredients in cooker including garlic, tomatoes, onion and water. Mix these ingredients with a wooden spatula and set your slow cooker to low setting for almost six hours.

Once the chicken is ready, use two forks to shred chicken and mix all vegetables and shredded chicken well. Serve with your favorite vegetables and lettuce leaves. Make sure to squeeze one lemon over chicken.

Spinach Frittata

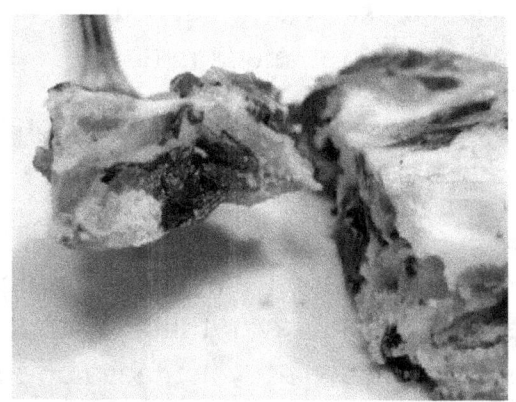

You can enjoy this healthy Frittata in breakfast or with evening tea. You can serve it in party as a snack.

Cooking Time: 1 ½ to 2 hours

Servings: 6

Ingredients:

- Olive oil (extra-virgin): 1 tablespoon
- Diced onion: 1/2 cup
- Mozzarella cheese (Shredded and divided): 1 cup
- Eggs: 3
- Egg whites: 3
- 1% milk: 2 tablespoons
- Black pepper: 1/4 teaspoon
- White pepper: 1/4 teaspoon
- Baby Spinach (chopped and remove stems): 1 cup

- Diced Roma tomato: 1
- Salt as per taste

Cooking Instructions:

Take one small skillet and add oil to sauté onion for almost five minutes on medium flame.

Grease your slow cooker with cooking spray and keep it aside.

Take one large bowl and mix sautéed onion, mozzarella cheese (3/4 cup) and all remaining ingredients. Whisk them well to combine everything and put them in the slow cooker. Sprinkle leftover cheese on the top of this mixture and cover your slow cooker. Cook this blend for almost 1 to 1 ½ hours on low setting. You can insert a knife in the middle to check either it is done. If the knife is clean, your frittata is ready. Cut into slices and serve hot.

Roast Beef

This can be a side dish or a full meal because of its delicious taste. You can cook everything in slow cooker easily.

Cooking Time: 8 to 10 hours

Servings: 4

Ingredients:

- Beef boneless (Chuck Roast): 3 lbs.
- Sweet Potatoes: 2 – 3 (cut big pieces)
- Carrots (cut big pieces): 4
- Sliced Onion: 1
- Fresh rosemary: 2 sprigs
- Bay leaves: 2
- Minced garlic: 2 cloves
- Red wine: 1 cup
- Balsamic Vinegar: 1/3 cup
- Beef stock: 1 ½ cup
- Coconut Oil: 2 tablespoons

- Black pepper (ground) and sea salt as per taste

Cooking Instructions:

Sprinkle black pepper and sea salt on the roast and keep it aside.

Melt coconut oil over medium heat in one large skillet and cook roast in this skillet for almost 2 to 3 minutes.

Put this meat in your slow cooker and top with all other ingredients. Cover your cooker and cook meat for nearly six hours on low setting.

Now add sweet potatoes and carrots in the slow cooker and cook for nearly three hours on high setting to tender vegetable and meat. Shred meat with two forks.

Discard rosemary sprigs and bay leaves and pour liquid in the slow cooker in one saucepan. Let it boil on medium heat and keep cooking until it reduces and become thick. Pour this sauce back in your slow cooker and serve with vegetables and meat.

Spicy Chicken

This delicious recipe has lots of health benefits because the chicken is a good source of protein.

Cooking Time: 4 to 6 hours

Servings: 4

Ingredients:

- Chicken pieces (remove skin): 2 to 3 lbs.
- Ground Ginger: 1 teaspoon
- Chipotle Pepper (ground): 1 teaspoon
- Curry Powder (yellow): 2 teaspoons
- Paprika: 1 teaspoon
- Garlic Powder: 1 teaspoon
- Ground Coriander: ½ teaspoon
- Ground Cardamom: ¼ teaspoon
- Ground cloves: 1/8 teaspoon
- Cayenne Pepper (ground): ¼ teaspoon

- Ground cumin: ½ teaspoon
- Black pepper (ground) and Salt
- Cooking fat (Paleo Fat)
- Onion (sliced): 1 large

Cooking Instructions:

Take one bowl and combine chipotle, pepper, ginger, salt, cayenne, cloves, cumin, cardamom, coriander, garlic powder, paprika and curry powder in this bowl. Mix them well and rub your chicken pieces with these spices.

Grease your slow cooker and put onion slices in the bottom. Place seasoned chicken pieces over onions and cover your slow cooker. Set it to a low setting to cook for almost 4 to 6 hours to tender chicken.

You can serve with chicken with your favorite sauce.

Chapter 3 – Paleo Stews and Soup Recipes

Slow cooking will prove helpful for soups and stews. There are some delicious Paleo soups and stews recipes that you can try at the dinner.

Vegetable Curry/Korma

This curry is free from added sugars, oils and fats and you can enjoy its flavor without any tension.

Cooking Time: 8 hours

Servings: 4 to 6

Ingredients:

- Cauliflower (break into florets): 1 large
- Chopped carrots: 2 large
- Green peas: 1/2 cup
- Chopped Green beans: 1 cup
- Chopped onion: 1/2 large
- Minced garlic: 2 cloves
- Coconut milk: 1 cup
- Curry powder: 2 tablespoon
- Sea salt: 1 tablespoon
- Garam masala: 1 teaspoon
- Red-pepper flakes: 1 tablespoon
- Almond meal: 2 tablespoons

Cooking Instructions:

Take your slow cooker and add chopped vegetables, garlic, and onion and mix all vegetables well.

Take one bowl and mix curry powder, coconut milk, garam masala, red-pepper flakes and sea salt in this bowl. Pour this mixture over vegetables and mix in almond meal. Mix them well and add any leftover ingredient in the slow cooker.

Cover your cooker and cook for eight hours on low setting and 5 hours on high setting to make the mixture thick. Serve this mixture immediately or secure in your fridge.

Lamb Stew

You can enjoy this spicy stew after a tiring day because slow cooker will do your work. Just put your ingredients and let the cooker do its work.

Cooking Time: 8 hours 10 minutes

Servings: 4 to 6

Ingredients:

- Lamb (diced): 2 lb.
- Spice Blend (Ras-El-Hanout): 4 tablespoons
- Diced Sweet Potatoes (peeled): 2
- Diced Apricots: 1 cup
- Diced bell pepper (red): 1
- Crushed tomatoes: 4 to 6
- Coconut Oil or Butter: 3 tablespoons

Cooking Instructions:

Take a dry and put it on the flame to roast your spice blend on hot and dry frying pan. Add lamb in the slow cooker and put all spices to coat each and every piece of lamb. Add butter and rest of the ingredients in slow cooker and mix them well. Set your slow cooker on low setting for 7 to 8 hours and cover it to cook stew. You can serve the stew with brown rice.

Beef Stew

This will be a comfortable meal in the night with salad and brown rice. You can serve this to your family at dinner.

Cooking Time: 8 hours 10 minutes

Servings: 5

Ingredients:

- Pastured beef (stewing): 2 pounds
- Beef stock: 2 cups
- Balsamic vinegar: 1 tablespoon
- Chopped onion: 1 medium
- Chopped Celery: 2 stalks
- Chopped carrots: 2 large
- Cubed potatoes: 3 to 5
- Minced garlic: 3 cloves
- Paprika: 1 Tablespoon

- Bay leaves: 3
- Salt: 1/2 teaspoon
- Black pepper: 1/2 teaspoon
- Dried rosemary, oregano and basil: 1 teaspoon each
- Arrowroot powder (to make stew thick): 1/8 cup

Cooking Instructions:

Put your meat in slow cooker and add all ingredients except arrowroot powder on the top of meat. Cover slow cooker and cook for eight hours on low setting. If you want to make it thick, you have to take out maximum liquid after completing eight hours and put this liquid in one saucepan. Let it boil and put some liquid in one small bowl and mix in arrowroot powder.

Whisk it well and add in the boiling liquid cooking in the saucepan. Make sure to whisk it well to avoid any lumps. Turn off heat and there is no need to reheat after adding arrowroot powder. It can break the thick bond of your stew. If your gravy is not thick as per your requirements, you can add more arrowroot powder. Pour this thick sauce back in the slow cooker, mix gently and serve.

Chicken Tortilla Soup

It is a quick and perfect dinner for weeknight after a busy and tiring day. Make in your slow cooker without extra efforts.

Cooking Time: 4 hours

Servings: 4 to 6

Ingredients:

- Olive oil: 2 Tablespoon
- Diced yellow onion: 1
- Diced bell pepper (red): 1
- Diced jalapeño: 1
- Minced garlic: 3 cloves
- Chicken (boneless and skinless): 3 to 4 breast
- Diced tomatoes: 28 ounce
- Green chile (diced): 4 ounce
- Chicken broth: 4 cups
- Chili powder: 2 teaspoons

- Ground cumin: 1 teaspoon
- Black pepper: As per taste
- Tortilla (cut small strips): 2 to 3
- Garnishing
- Cilantro (chopped)
- Guacamole

Cooking Instructions:

Preheat oil in one skillet on medium heat and sauté jalapeno, bell pepper, garlic and onion to make onions translucent. Put all these cooked vegetables in slow cooker and add remaining includes (except guacamole, tortilla and cilantro). Cook for almost 4 hours on high setting and 8 hours on low settings.

After cooking, remove chicken with the help of tongs and put on a plate or cutting board. Use 2 forks or even knife to shred chicken pieces into small bite-sized pieces. Add chicken back in your slow cooker and mix all ingredients well along with tortilla strips. Serve with guacamole and cilantro garnishing.

Vegetable and Beans Soup

You can enjoy this delicious soup by adding your favorite vegetables and some beans. It can be a handy addition to your diet.

Cooking Time: 4 to 8 hours

Servings: 6

Ingredients:

- Green beans (chopped): 1 cup
- Carrots (Sliced): 4
- Red potato (cubed): 1 large
- Celery (chopped): 2 ribs
- Sweet onion (diced): 1/2 cup
- Corn kernels: 1 cup
- Paprika: 1 teaspoon
- Sea salt: 1/2 teaspoon
- Black pepper: 1/2 teaspoon
- Allspice: 1/8 teaspoon
- Diced tomatoes: 15 ounce
- Vegetable broth (without fat): 2 cups

- Olive oil (extra-virgin): 1 teaspoon
- Northern beans (drained): 15 ounce

Cooking Instructions:

Add all these ingredients to your slow cooker and mix them well to combine everything. Cover your cooker and cook on low setting for eight hours to tender carrots. If you want to cook on high setting, you have to cook for almost 4 hours.

In the last hour of cooking, you can remove ½ ingredients and mash them well with the help of one fork. Put these mashed ingredients in the slow cooker again and mix them well and continue cooking. It proves helpful to make your soup thick.

Chapter 4 – Paleo Chicken Recipes in Slow Cooker

There are lots of delicious recipes to cook chicken in slow cooker. With the help of these recipes, you can serve yummy meals to your family.

Salsa Chicken

This moist and delicious chicken is easy to prepare in slow cooker. You can get the advantage of some spices.

Cooking Time: 6 to 7 hours

Servings: 4

Ingredients:

- Chicken (remove fat and skin): 4 Breasts
- Green Mild Salsa: 16oz
- Water: ⅓ Cup
- Dried Parsley: 1½ Tablespoons
- Dried Cilantro: ½ Tablespoon
- Onion Powder: 1 Teaspoon
- Garlic Powder: 1 Teaspoon
- Dried Oregano: ½ Tablespoon
- Smoked Paprika: ½ Teaspoon
- Cumin: ½ Teaspoon
- Chili Powder: 1 Teaspoon

- Black Pepper: ¼ Teaspoon

Cooking Instructions:

Put chicken pieces in the bottom of your slow cooker and add rest of the ingredients on its top. Mix them well and cover this cook. Cook on low setting for almost 6 to 7 hours.

Chicken Cacciatore

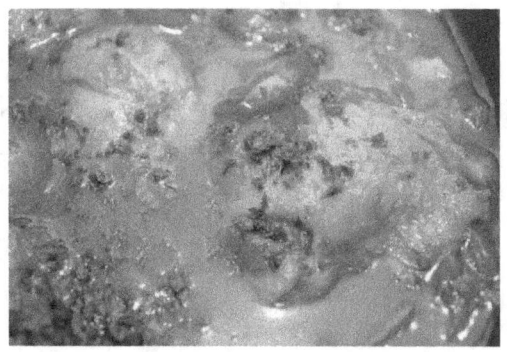

This Chicken Cacciatore is really delicious and you can get the advantage of this delicious recipe.

Cooking Time: 6 hours 15 minutes

Servings: 4 to 6

Ingredients:

- Coconut oil: 2 Tablespoons
- Minced onion: 1 large
- Tomato paste: 1/4 cup
- Dried oregano: 1 1/2 teaspoons
- Minced garlic: 2 to 3 cloves
- Red pepper (flakes): 1/4 teaspoon
- Diced tomatoes: 15 ounce
- Chicken stock: 1/2 cup
- White mushrooms (quartered): 2 lb.

- Red wine: 1/2 cup

Cooking Instructions:

Take a pan and cook tomato paste, garlic, flakes of red pepper, oregano, and onion along with coconut oil in this pan. Put this mixture in your slow cooker and mix in chicken stock, tomatoes, wine, and mushrooms. Season pieces of chicken with pepper and salt and add them to your slow cooker. Mix each and everything together, cover your cooler and cook on low setting for almost 4 to 6 hours.

Roast Chicken

It is easy to make roast chicken in your slow cooker. You can get the advantage of this delicious recipe.

Cooking Time: 4 hours 5 minutes

Servings: 6

Ingredients:

- Whole chicken: 4-to-6 pound
- Yellow onion: 1
- Garlic: 1 head
- Lemon or orange: 1
- Paprika: 1 tablespoon
- Sea salt: 2 teaspoon
- Pepper: 2 teaspoon
- Dried thyme: 1 teaspoon
- Kitchen twine: 8 inches

- Carrots, celery or parsnips: 2

Cooking Instructions:

Quarter your lemon and onion, and cut the garlic head by cutting it from the middle.

Take a bowl and mix pepper, thyme and salt in this bowl.

Put celery, parsnips or carrots in the bottom of your slow cooker and put your chicken in the slow cooker. Sprinkle some salt mixture in the cavity of chicken and rub rest of the mixture on the top of your chicken. Sprinkle rest of the ingredients on chicken and close the lid of your slow cooker. You have to cook on high for almost four hours. You can cut the chicken into slices after cooking to serve.

Chicken Chili

This chili is easy and delicious for everyone. You can serve chili at dinner because your family will like it.

Cooking Time: 7 hours 5 minutes

Servings: 4 to 6

Ingredients:

- Chicken thighs (Boneless and skinless): 8 to 12
- Salsa: 16-ounce
- Italian tomatoes (diced): 16-ounce
- Chopped yellow onion: 1 medium
- Chopped red pepper: 1 large
- Chili powder: 2 tablespoons

Cooking Instructions:

Roughly chop chicken to make 1-inch pieces and put them in your slow cooker. Pour all remaining ingredients in the cooker and mix them well and put the lid on it. Set slow cooker on high for almost 4 to 6 hours and low for 6 to 8 hours. Serve with lettuce leaf or brow rice.

Chicken and Mushroom Gravy

Mushroom and chicken gravy offers unique flavor and filling meal. This recipe is easy with your slow cooker.

Cooking Time: 4 hours

Servings: 5

Ingredients:

- Chicken fillets (skinless): 1 1/2 pounds
- Canola oil: 2 tablespoons
- Crimini mushrooms (sliced): 16 ounces
- Yellow onion (thin slices): 1
- Minced garlic: 2 cloves
- Black pepper: 1/2 teaspoon
- Sea salt as per taste
- Chopped leaf parsley: 1/4 cup
- Chicken broth (without fat and sodium): 1 1/2 cups
- Cornstarch: 2 tablespoons

Cooking Instructions:

Add oil in slow cooker and rest of the ingredients in your slow cooker. Cover this slow cooker and set on a low setting to cook for almost 3.5 to 4.5 hours. Remove chicken and keep it aside. It is time to add cornstarch in your slow cooker and cook for almost 15 minutes. Add chicken again and mix them well. You can serve it with pasta and brown rice.

Chapter 5 – Paleo Dessert Recipes

You can prepare delicious desserts with the help of these recipes. These delicious and simple recipes are easy to try for everyone.

Glazed Pecans

You can use this recipe to glaze pecans and even other nuts, such as almond and walnut. It will be a good way to give a unique flavor to nuts.

Cooking Time: 2 hours 10 minutes

Servings: 6

Ingredients:

- Raw pecans: 3 cups
- Maple syrup: ¼ cup
- Vanilla beans (ground): 2 teaspoons
- Sea salt: 1 teaspoon
- Coconut oil: 1 tablespoon

Cooking Instructions:

Put all these ingredients in your slow cooker and cook for almost 1 to 3 hours on low setting. Make sure to mix often. Let them cool down and store these pecans in one Mason jar.

Apple Pie Sauce

You can enjoy this sauce with your favorite ice cream or even cookies. This will be a great combination for everyone.

Cooking Time: 4 hours 15 minutes

Servings: 6

Ingredients:

- Coconut oil: ⅓ cup
- Lemon juice: 1 tablespoon
- Cane juice (evaporated): ¼ cup
- Cinnamon powder: ½ teaspoon
- Vanilla extract: 1 teaspoon
- Sea salt: ½ teaspoon
- Apples (remove skin and cored): 6 medium (cut into 1" cubes)

Cooking Instructions:

Whisk all ingredients together and put in slow cooker. Cover your slow cooker and cook on high setting for four hours. You can serve it hot or cold as per your needs.

Brownie Bites

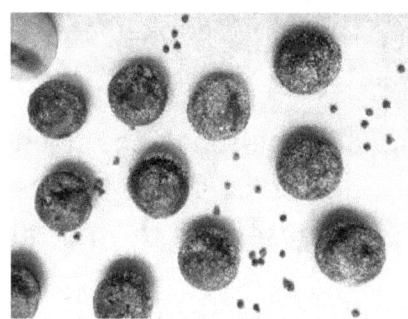

Enjoy brownies bites by making them in slow cooker. You can make them from scratch.

Cooking Time: 4 hours 30 minutes

Servings: 10

Ingredients:

- Almond flour (blanched): 2 cups
- Coconut sugar: 1 cup
- Cocoa powder (unsweetened): 3/4 cup
- Baking powder: 2 teaspoons
- Baking soda: 2 teaspoons
- Salt: 1 teaspoon
- Eggs: 2
- Coconut milk (unsweetened): 1/2 cup
- Coconut oil (melted): 1/2 cup
- Vanilla extract (pure): 2 teaspoons
- Brewed coffee: 1/3 cup

Cooking Instructions:

Grease your slow cooker with oil.

Mix all ingredients and spread them in the slow cooker equally. Cover this slow cooker and cooker for 4 to 5 hours on low setting.

After cooking brownies, let them cool for almost ½ hour and use one cookie scoop to scoop out and make small balls. Serve these balls to your family.

Beef Tongue with Roasted Pepper Sauce

Ingredients

Tongue:

1 Beef Tongue

1 Onion - sliced

3 Garlic Cloves - crushed

3 Bay Leaves

Sea Salt and Black Pepper – for taste

Water to cover Tongue in slow cooker

Sauce:

1 Roasted Red Pepper - peeled and diced

1 Roasted Serrano Chili Pepper - diced

1 Onion - diced

3 Garlic Cloves - minced

20oz Tomatoes - sliced

6oz tomato puree

1 Teaspoon Thyme

1 Teaspoon Oregano

Sea Salt and Black Pepper - to taste

Directions

Tongue:

Place the onion, garlic and bay leaves at the bottom of the slow cooker.

Add the beef tongue on top and season generously with salt and pepper. Submerge the tongue in water and cook on low for 8 hours.

Remove the tongue from the cooker and peel off the skin. Shred with a fork and serve with the sauce.

Sauce:

In a pan, sauté the onions, garlic, red pepper and serrano chili until the onions are translucent.

Combine with all the other ingredients and stir thoroughly.

Simmer for 30 minutes and serve with the shredded tongue.

Bouef Bourgignon

Serves 4-6

Ingredients

2lbs Grass-fed Beef Stew Meat

1 Large Onion - chopped

2 Garlic Cloves - chopped

2 Large Carrots - peeled and sliced

1 Small Turnip - peeled and diced

3 Sprigs fresh Rosemary

2 Bay Leaves

1 Teaspoon Sea Salt

1 Teaspoon Black Pepper

2 Tablespoon Dijon Mustard

2 Cups Beef Stock

1/4 Cup Red Wine Vinegar

1/2lb Mushrooms - sliced

2 Tablespoons Water

Directions

Season the beef with salt and pepper.

In a heated pan, cook the beef and brown off the edges.

When the meat is cooked, transfer beef to a plate and in the plan sauté the onion and garlic until the onion is translucent.

Add the red wine vinegar, Dijon mustard and bring to a simmer. Transfer all ingredients to the slow cooker. Add in the carrots, turnips, mushrooms, rosemary and bay leaves. Cook on low for 8 hours.

When the meat is cooked through, remove the beef, strain off the juice and serve on top.

Braised Lamb Shanks & Eggplant

Serves 4

Ingredients

1.5lb Eggplant - peeled

4 x 12 oz. Lamb Shanks - trimmed

2 Tablespoons Ground Sumac

1.5 Teaspoons Salt

½ Teaspoon freshly Ground Pepper

2 Tablespoon Extra Virgin Olive Oil

1 Large Green Bell Pepper - diced

1 Small Onion - diced

3 Garlic Cloves - minced

5 Plum Tomatoes - diced

1 Cup Water

½ Cup Parsley – finely chopped

Directions

Slice the eggplant lengthwise in half-inch wide slices, then width-way in 1 inch chunks and set aside.

Rub lamb shanks with the sumac and season with salt and pepper.

In a pan, heat 1 tablespoon of oil over a medium heat and cook the lamb until brown all over (5-7 mins). Transfer lamb to a plate and more oil to the pan, along with the bell pepper, onion, garlic and remaining sumac. Cook until vegetables begin to soften.

Add the lamb and the vegetables to the slow cooker and add in the eggplant, tomatoes and water, and cook on high for 2 hours or until the lamb becomes tender.

Add the parsley and cook for 5-10 more minutes and then serve.

Breakfast Frittata

Ingredients

3/4 Cups frozen Spinach - thawed and squeezed dry

1.5 Cups Red Bell Pepper - diced

1/4 Cups Red Onion - diced

8 Large Eggs - beaten

1/2 Teaspoon Black Pepper

1 Teaspoon Sea Salt

1.5 Cups Sausage

Directions

In a pre-heated pan, add the sausage and brown off.

Combine the spinach, red pepper, onions, eggs, salt and pepper and sausage in a slow cooker and stir thoroughly.

Cook on medium heat for 2-3 hours or until the frittata becomes well set.

Serve and enjoy.

Butternut Squash Soup

Serves 4-6

Ingredients

6 Cups Butternut Squash - chopped

2 Medium Apples - peeled, cored and chopped

2 Medium Carrots - peeled and chopped

1 Small White Onion –peeled and chopped

1 Garlic Clove – crushed

2 Cups Chicken Stock

1/2 Teaspoon dried Sage

1.5 Teaspoons dried Thyme

1/2 Teaspoon Sea Salt

1/4 Teaspoon ground Black Pepper

1 Cup Almond Milk

Topping

6 Slices of Bacon - cooked and crumbled

Handful of Parsley - chopped

Directions

Place the squash, apples, onions, carrots, garlic and stock in the slow cooker and cook on low for 6-8 hours.

Add in the almond milk and stir thoroughly. Transfer the ingredients to a blender and blend until smooth.

Season with salt and pepper to taste if desired Serve with the chopped bacon and parsley.

Carnitas on Red Pepper Nachos

Ingredients

3.5lb Pork Roast

1 Teaspoon of Sea salt and Black Pepper

2 Tablespoons Olive Oil

1 Teaspoon dried Thyme

4 Bay Leaves

1 Cup of Chicken Stock

Directions

Roll the pork roast and coat with salt and pepper.

Heat a tablespoon of oil in a skillet and brown the pork.

Add the pork, along with all the other ingredients to the slow cooker and cook on low for 6-8 hours.

Roasted Pepper Nachos

Ingredients

4 Small Sweet Peppers - halved

Filling of your choice

Directions

Stuff the peppers with carnitas and bake for 10 min at 350 degrees.

Sweet Potato Mash with Pecans

Ingredients

2lb Sweet Potatoes - peeled and cut into 1/2 inch slices

1 Cup Apple Juice

1 Tablespoon Ground Cinnamon

1 Teaspoon Ground Nutmeg

1/2 Teaspoon Allspice

1/4 Teaspoon Ground Cloves

After cooking stir in

Cinnamon and Nutmeg to taste

Apple Juice

Pecans

1 Tablespoon of Raw Honey or Maple Syrup

Directions

Prepare the sweet potatoes and place in the slow cooker with half a cup of apple juice and all the spices and cook for 4-5 hours, until potatoes are tender.

When the potatoes are cooked through, add the ingredients to a blender and blend until smooth.

Season with cinnamon and nutmeg and serve.

Cauliflower Mashed Potatoes with Garlic & Dill

Ingredients

1 Large head of Cauliflower.

6 Garlic Cloves

1/3 Cup fresh Dill - chopped.

1 Teaspoon of Sea Salt and Black Pepper

Splash or Coconut Milk

6 Cups of Water

Directions

Remove the leaves and stem of the cauliflower and cut the head into florets and place into the slow cooker. Add garlic and half of the dill.

Add the water to the slow cooker and cover the cauliflower and cook on high for 4-5 hours.

Allow the slow cooker to cool and drain the contents into a colander. Remove the dill from the mixture and place the cauliflower into a bowl.

Add salt and pepper to taste, along with the remaining freshly chopped dill and the coconut milk and puree with an immersion blender (or a food blender if preferred).

Garnish with more fresh dill and serve.

Celery Hearts with Creamed Kale

Serves 2

Ingredients

2 Carrots - chopped

3 Celery Hearts - chopped

1 Onion - chopped

2 Garlic Cloves - crushed

3 Jalapenos – chopped and seeded

3/4 cup Coconut Flakes

1 Teaspoon Cayenne Powder

1 Teaspoon Chilli Powder

1 Teaspoon Red Pepper

1 Teaspoon Smoked Paprika

1/2 Teaspoon Allspice

1/2 teaspoon Cloves

2 Teaspoons Cilantro Flakes

1 Large bunch of Kale - sliced

1/2 Can of Coconut Milk

Directions

Cut the hearts in half and remove valves and connective fibres.

Place the carrot, onion, garlic, jalapenos, coconut flakes, spices in the bottom of the slow cooker.

Place the heart in the middle of the slow cooker and cover with the remaining vegetables. Add a cup of water or stock and cook on low for 6 hours.

When the heart is cooked through, place the kale in a pan and pour in the coconut milk and sauté until the kale is soft.

Slice the heart into small pieces and serve over kale.

Cheater's Pork Stew

Serves 4-6

Ingredients

2 Small Onions - thinly sliced

6 Garlic Cloves - peeled and crushed

1/2lb Baby Carrots

1 Teaspoon Kosher Salt

1 Teaspoon freshly ground Black Pepper

3lbs Pork Shoulder - cut into 1.5 inch cubes

1 Tablespoon of your favourite seasoning

1 Tablespoon Fish Sauce

1 Small Cabbage - cut into 8 wedges

1 Cup Marinara Sauce

1 Tablespoon Balsamic Vinegar

1/4 Cup Parsley - finely chopped

Directions

Peel and slice the onion and peel and crush the garlic cloves. Place them in the slow cooker with the carrots and season with salt and pepper.

Slice the pork into cubes and season with the fish sauce and your favourite seasoning and place the pork in the slow cooker on top of the vegetables. Tuck the cabbage wedges on top and drizzle the marinara sauce on top and season with more salt and pepper. Cook on low for 8-10 hours.

When the vegetables are tender, add in the balsamic vinegar and top with fresh parsley.

Conclusion

Paleo diet includes consumption of fruits, roots, meat, nuts and organ meats. You have to exclude grains, processed oils, dairy products, sugar, legumes, coffee, salt, and alcohol. You should avoid modern processed foods and harmful food that can increase your weight. It will be good to consume chicken, grass-fed meat, duck, hen, turkey, and wild fish.

This diet restricts the use of processed food, preservatives, toxic food and whole grains. These foods can destroy your health, and this diet can save you from all caveats of a modern lifestyle. It will help you to manage stress in your life, build muscles, reduce risks of kidney and heart diseases, boost your immune system and improve your sleeping habits by regulating body clock. It will help you to get a firm and healthy body. It is good to reduce your weight and improve your overall health.

You can try lots of delicious recipes that are easy to prepare in the slow cooker. These methods enable you to satisfy your craving without sacrificing your taste. These may not increase your weight, but you can enjoy them as per their points. In the paleo diet, you will get a few points by your weight and body mass. You have to follow them before eating anything. This book has

25 slow cooker recipes with their points. You can try them quickly.

www.ingramcontent.com/pod-product-compliance
Lightning Source LLC
Chambersburg PA
CBHW071450070526
44578CB00001B/295